The Broken Branch Grows

~ poeticized writings in verse ~

B. Kay Mackle

First published in Far North Queensland, 2024 by Bowerbird Publishing

@ 2024 B. Kay Mackle

ISBN 978-0-6486041-8-1 (paperback)
ISBN 978-0-7635643-0-5 (ebook)

The Broken Branch Grows
Poeticized Writings in Verse
B. Kay Mackle

First edition: 2024

Edited by: Crystal Leonardi, Bowerbird Publishing
Interior Design by: Crystal Leonardi, Bowerbird Publishing
Cover Design by: Crystal Leonardi, Bowerbird Publishing

Distributed by Bowerbird Publishing
Available in National Library of Australia

Bowerbird Publishing
Julatten, Queensland, Australia
www.crystalleonardi.com

In honour of my parents, knowing they did the best that they could, believing they could have done better.

For the love of my family, knowing I did the best that I could, believing I also could have done better.

That is the way.

ABOUT THE AUTHOR

B. Kay Mackle is passionate about her soul mission.

Her dedication to children's wellbeing and life education shines through her words and stories. The narrative is not just stories, but powerful tools that can shape young minds with messages waiting to be discovered on every page.

Kay's stories are written to encourage parents, grandparents, and teachers to read aloud to children, fostering the return of 'story time.'

Kay emphasises the Power of Three:

Reading leads to **Education**

Reading generates **Knowledge**

Reading creates **Experience**

Kay believes that reading produces power and asks students of all ages to return to spelling, for teachers to look at changing the curriculum and revisit the power of repetition.

OTHER TITLES BY B. KAY MACKLE

~ The Power of Three: Dakness to Light

~ Stepping Stones: Walk the Path

For more information on these titles,

please email kaym@internode.on.net

Clarification to Bring to Light

A recollection of events,
A voyage of separation,
In preparation for a life cycle of growth.
A new way to advance,
As a broken branch,
A new way of living
MY LIFE.

A Source of attraction leads me on,
A light so bright it cannot be ignored.
Never before has my existence mattered,
All matters addressed, now is the time to be as best.
A Time to invest,
Trusted and true,
A new path awaits the authentic self.

T he Broken Branch Grows

T*he Broken Branch Grows*

Growth

Time can always heal the hurt,
Time can always heal the pain.
You must be willing to do the work,
You have the most to gain.
Separate, different, pulling away,
Knowing you have to stay,
Knowing you have more to say.
The saying goes, forgive and forget,
The reality is, without forgiving you have regret.
You never forget,
You learn not to get upset.
The act of forgiving sets you free,
Setting a new example to be.
New pathways open up,
New shoots show green and healing.
New growth, new life buds,
FREEDOM to bloom and be seen
Somewhere, other than the kitchen sink.
There are new beginnings, it seems,
This is the time to move forward.
The love of flowers grows,
A new beauty,
Peace from within it shows.

Fright

Uncertain - the curtain is drawn – dark
Back into rejection and loss – grey
Nothing to fear – awaken – gaze ahead
Lead light windows of colour – blue
Unveil the new healing light – green

Butterfly wishes sent on high,
Light up the sky at night.
Like stars so brilliant so bright – white
You were right to question the cage of darkness,
That now leads to the light of a new day.

Grounding

The calm waters become unsettled,
The balance is disrupted.
Stay focused, stay still in the mind,
Let the rhythm settle in the heart.
As the waves beat onto the shore,
Restore the emotion, breathe, relax.
Centre self in awareness, peace.
Dissolve the issues at hand,
Reinforce your beliefs of body, mind and spirit.
Regain balance on land,
Life is in your hands,
And so, it is.

Poetic Justice

Keeping balanced on the waves – tumble.
Turbulence rises from underneath,
The sands are shifting below.
Struggling to keep upright,
Feet are firmly grounded.
Roots are spread deep,
Do not accept defeat.
As the heat rises to the surface,
The arms are open wide.
The intention was to fly,
The struggle, now, to keep afloat.
As eyes are open to the wind,
The water gently settles.
It is just a matter of time,
Before the sun and moon exchange places.
The energy rises,
These are signs of the times.

Disbelief

An episode of doubt,
An investment - an intention.
A trigger - a raised voice,
Reduced to heavy heart.
A blockage – baggage – rewind,
Let go – return to the present.
Mind control – let it roll,
Old energy – a small hurdle.
Take the jump to the other side,
Belief – trust.
Self-conflict swept aside,
Walk by my side with intention.
A round – about control,
Focus and soften the stare.
Look with new eyes,
New ways to address this situation.
New energy – new thoughts – a bridge,
Return to the heart,
Return – choose love; above all other.

The Broken Branch Grows

Daybreak

Breaking through — New Earth.
A softening of the surface,
Time to face the World.
Time to uncurl and heal the wounds,
Shift the perspective — a learning curve.
A happening — a different view,
Never a mountain, a hill of sand,
Always changing at will.
Reducing the strain and the struggle,
Inspired by the butterfly.
A process of change,
Never out of range.
Connecting the pieces,
The colours — a gift alone.
Never a stone,
A rock to hold onto.
Strong, determined, focused,
A life now inspired
By colour and light.

B. Kay Mackle

Exchange

Destination unknown,
Travelling without a phone,
The coast is clear,
The road is long.
The map is in my head,
The knowing is in my heart.
Trusting my journey until the end,
Around every bend I see differences.
The colour of the landscape blend,
An aura of blue - uplifting sky,
A white cloud drifting by.
A land – a sea of green and gold,
I see a new path about to begin.
Listening, I hear nature calling,
The bush birds that cry,
A reminder they need protection.
An eye – of consciousness – aware,
Connection to All – Creation,
The wings of change.

Master Task

Uncharted waters,
Lead me on.
A river flows directly to the sea,
See what is before you.
Be the captain,
Be the anchor,
Hold the mask high,
The sky is the limit.
Bow to the creator of all there is,
Anything is possible,
The years are passing.
The waves have led you here,
You are now ready to receive your blessings.
Are you ready to talk?
Are you ready to walk?
Are you ready to set sail?
What do you have for sale?
What are your daily needs?
Crystals and beads or food shelter and water?

Blood Line

Softly spoken words of foreign tongue,
Made aware of spiritual presence.
Massage of the nose, eyes and ears,
A book, a passage.
Nature of the supreme,
An energetic force.
Conscious of body and mind,
A part and as a whole.
The soul presence,
A spiritual spark divided,
Influences the spirit soul,
A heart influenced by the sun.
A soul maintained by regal blood,
To acknowledge the supreme personality of Godhead.

Buying Time

Moments, precious moments
pass by,
Lingering only to catch your eye.
Past – gone – never to be replaced,
As the sun rises on high,
The shadows fade.
A place in time,
One breath – one sigh,
The past has served its purpose.
The future – a distant line of communication,
Awareness – stop – listen – silence,
Breathe.
First breath ----- last breath,
Death comes to all.
In one moment,
Life is gone,
Catch each breath as it passes.

Expression

Footprints – pressed gently into the surface,
Visible until the winds and the tide turn.
Turn around – find no impression,
Washed and blown away.
The earth remembers every stride,
Pride is accomplished by being real.
Softly touched for a second,
A second chance to show and tell.
Mysteries from long past,
Never forgotten – never lost.
Stories unfold – love letters,
Written on the land.
Band together – to benefit,
All of mankind,
A universal exchange.

The Broken Branch Grows

A Chance Meeting

Come back to me my heart,
You were with me in my younger years.
I let you go and only remember the tears,
Shed for another life – and love.
I remember in my soul,
A soul yearning,
Years of learning,
Little steps I progressed.
Forgetting the pain of losing you,
I stumble on to find.
You have been with me all the time,
I only had to accept love into my heart,
Forgive me for letting you go.

A Time and Place

Young years waisted,

Youth depleted.

Hurts and pains forgiven — never repeated.

Hear the praises of the child,

A modern word disposed.

Rise again my friend,

Rise and seek mercy.

Cannot see with present eyes,

The mystic sees with Divine eyes.

The future is here in one place,

Lovingly received and lovingly exchanged.

Completely arranged,

Loving in degrees of faith and humility.

A seed once planted,

Now grows in faith.

From whence arose a family tree.

The Broken Branch Grows

As It Is

Angels calling a ringing in my ear,
A shift is happening the words are clear.
The puzzle pieces are presented,
The space is smaller the pieces fit.
The sand script language explains,
The heart is open to respond.
The heart is open to the gift,
A gift of prophecy.
A gift – a jewel – a crown,
A rule of existence.
A prayer awakens the soul,
The soul never dies.
The awakening is upon us,
Divine intervention brings
Peace to Earth.

Re cycle

The original sin creates,
Brings life ever-after.
Trappings of the skin,
Trappings of the heart.
Soul reactions unfold,
Someone to hold.
Truths untold,
Telling secrets,
Hidden secrets,
As yet to be told.
Lust not loves,
A heavenly intervention.
Not the intention,
Only a way out.
To begin a new life of trust,
A beginning to a new cycle of life.

The Broken Branch Grows

Being Real

A moment of reflection
Brings hope,
A mindful state of being
Brings joy,
Inspired to create happiness,
Fate in understanding.
Messages of power,
Encourage success.
Revel in love,
A real state of being.

Forgiveness

Different faces,

Different races,

Same recognition of the heart.

Blood is blood,

Water is water,

Bring the attention to the table.

Needs and desires,

Opportunities – fires,

In justice – serve.

Questions – answers,

For the good of All.

Appreciate life,

Pause for what cause.

Power – control,

Ignorance at best,

Make a difference in defence.

Direction

Living on with the differences made,
Living life without the storm.
Fine-tuning – healing,
Perceived and past mistakes – revealing.
Lessons – not a lost cause,
A strategic plan of action.
A life plan – gaining knowledge,
Wise decisions – follow.
Instinctive wisdom – follow through,
New direction opens up.
A force greater than man,
A candidate for life.
A way show er – survives,

New Level

A still golden pond,
Reflected by the moon,
A golden lotus in bloom.
A magic wand is waved,
A new way is craved.
An opening,
A window of opportunity,
Time to act.
A circle – a spiral of love,
A gentle soul – detached.
Self-empowered and strong,
Stay firm – within boundaries of support.
Gifts from source,
See your role in society.

Remember

Free spirit,

Opening up with simplicity and grace.

Love is coming in degrees,

Love is by perception.

A state of bliss,

An unexpected kiss,

The wind in the trees.

A cloud passing by,

A beautiful flower,

A single lotus blossoms.

Sun light,

A string of pearls,

Love in mind heart and soul.

Raindrops on my shoulder,

A teardrop from heaven,

Guides me on,

Eternally yours.

The Final Note

An inside truth,

A girl of passion with her own fashion of speaking,

The truth.

She calls a truce,

She stops fighting herself,

She forgives herself.

She opens up to Gods wishes,

She has been offered bread and fishes.

The flood gates have been opened,

The sea of tears has at last parted.

Silenced for many years,

Her words had become tears.

Her faith had been shattered,

She hid in fear.

She returned to darkness although she craved the light,

She held on to anxiety for fear of defeat.

Her feet kept her grounded,

Her head was in the clouds circling around.

She kept her feelings to herself,

Her emotions - bubbled over.

She is over it - this darkness,

She craves THE LIGHT.

Consciousness

She faces her fears,

Letting go of fear she regains her strength.

She regains her courage,

She regains her faith; she believes in consciousness.

She has her vision,

No more prison. No more cages. No more walls.

She stands tall - a tall order.

This warrior spirit she suffers no more.

She is THE LIGHT,

She is LOVE.

She understands the meaning of LOVE.

Love will stand by YOU,

Love will show THE WAY,

Love will listen.

Now they will listen when she speaks,

For she has messages to tell THE WORLD.

The WRITTEN WORD SPEAKS VOLUMES,

She speaks her TRUTH.

Her story. Her reality. Her honesty.

Let her conscious be her guide (Jiminy Cricket)

Confirmation

Confirmation out-weighs growth.

She waits, not knowing her next step,

She has grown in so many ways.

Sometimes she is frightened,

Sometimes she is brave.

Always she behaves in the way she has been accustomed to,

Sometimes she ventures out-side to explore the evermore.

She knows there is more to life,

She knows there is more to learn.

She knows she has possibilities. So why the hesitation?

Why the wait? Why must she wait? What holds her back?

Who has her back? Who will protect her?

Who will save her if she fails or falls?

Faith is always the one to call on,

Faith is one to hold on to.

Faith has her back.

Way back she lost faith,

Now faith has been found.

Even if it has been on the rebound,

Faith is sound and secure; a proven resource.

Security is what is needed at this stage of life,

Validated and confirmed.

The Broken Branch Grows

Quintessence

An epitome. A realization. An insight.
Recognise the achievements that have been made.
Recognise the input,
Recognise the value,
Recognise the Spirit within.
Within each great being is a soul,
A sole purpose to achieve,
To be the best one can be.
To be authenticated,
To be valued,
To be noticed,
For one's worth.
Trust in the Lord and allow it to happen,
I have nothing to fear knowing you are near.
An essence of heart and soul,
Whole perfect and complete.

The Embrace of Time

From a stage of metamorphism,

Hidden from sight,

Alone in the darkness,

A sheltered life,

A protected life.

A jewel of life like no other,

shiny yellow and bright.

She emerges,

From a state of stillness,

she awakes,

From darkness to light.

She rises,

Dries her eyes and stretches her wings,

towards the welcoming sunshine,

bright and receiving.

Revealing the colour blue,

What awaits her?

What confronts her?

Where is she and where is she going?

Have faith young Butterfly,

Your wings will support you.

Your wings are strong,

The air, the breath, will guide you far and wide,

Your purpose is to survive.

LIVE by your word,

LIVE your life to the fullest,

Fly little butterfly, fly.

This blue that surrounds you is a different shade of blue,

a blue coat of protection,

showing the world,

your TRUE COLOUR.

By Choice

She chose to follow a path unknown,
She reached a bridge.
As the road had narrowed, she chose not to go back,
She chose to cross the bridge.
The bridge was high, it captured her heart,
She chose to climb the bridge.
As she reached the top,
She looked down to see her troubles starting to wash away,
and she decided to let them go.
She danced across the bridge to the other side,
not knowing what awaited her.
A brighter side of life with colours and light,
A sight to behold – rainbows.
Bringing silver, gold and diamond light,
She is seeing another world of friendship, love and hope.
A soul light - a gifted light,
A higher purpose is her right of passage.

Soul Desire

In souls defence I was relentless.
Less is now more,
More is now a projected vision,
A vision of fortitude and grace.
Time to pick up the pace,
Rarity in spirit,
more now than before.
Before you are possibilities, opportunities,
Time to take chances,
The options are endless.
Excitement is imminent,
Preparations are the order of the day.
What do you have to say?
What do you want to say?
Where will this happen?
Where will this take place?
A place of worship and praise,
A day of reconning,
On any given day,
A day to behold,
Your story must be told.
Face to face,
By the grace of God.

B. Kay Mackle

The Primary Factor

Self-awareness; brings attention.

Self-Love; the key to all disturbance.

Self-worth; the key to success.

Self-belief; opens the lock.

Confidence; opens the door.

Self-intention; brings least distraction.

Actions; speak louder than words.

Communication; is the x-factor.

The primary role; is to educate.

A role model; is you.

Body & Soul

Hear me (she cried),
Truth (not lies).
She heard the replies,
Surprised (she listened),
This was the way out of her prison (her mind).
An open mind (willing),
The way was to mend her broken heart,
Realize she had a choice to engage,
Understand herself,
Believe in herself,
Trust she was on the right path.
A path-way to LOVE,
Ground breaking news.
She has arrived,
Welcome her with open arms,
This bringer of joy to the world,
She deserves applause for all her hard work.
Her perseverance,
Her dedication,
Her beliefs,
Believe this story as it is the TRUTH.
Truth must be told,
Always.

B. Kay Mackle

Alliance

YOU can-not HIDE.
MEMORIES (fade),
TIME (heals).
DIVINE TIME (revealing),
EVOLUTION (progression),
SUCCESS (realization),
Failure (NOT AN OPTION).
OPPINION (matters),
ATTAINMENT (fulfilled),
ALIGNMENT (arranged),
POSITION (secure).
Paid in advance bulk-billed,
THE UNIVERSE (provides),
TOGETHER (we grow),
IN LOVE (we evolve),
IN UNITY (we advance).
Take a chance ON ME,
HONESTY (will prevail).

The Broken Branch Grows

Performance Shift

Side step to avoid the inevitable.

Cards on the table,

An open display,

Generous and sincere.

The ending is near,

Near and from afar,

Back and forth.

A force more powerful than your will,

The universe has your back.

The universe provides,

The is no lack of faith,

Lack of motivation perhaps?

Purpose filled,

A plan of action,

Reforming,

Aligning,

Balancing,

No acting.

Being real,

For the advantage of the masses.

Diamonds or Stones

Some days feel beyond repair,
cracks too deep to heal.
The spirit has been recognised,
The heart is held together with a bow.
The head wobbles on the spine,
What is, ones to keep?
The soul weeps,
the soul is wounded.
Neither here nor there,
struggling with the after birth.
Life is not always what one planned,
Life is not always what is expected.
A fall from grace to save face,
Face the facts of life.
Not good enough to love!
Who stood at the alter? Who was the judge?
Who qualifies? Who lay down? Who stayed down?
Who carried the frown and the pain
as the crown was broken?
Going around and around,
Finally finding a little happiness in the garden,
the rose slowly unfolds.

The Broken Branch Grows

The petals red and pink,

Changing from white no longer pure.

What more can one endure?

Choosing ones' own seed,

nurtured in warm earth.

Loved and sheltered,

growing and protected in green,

The petals do not open!

No yellow to be seen,

Yet to experience the feeling of joy before death,

Made perfect, dropped, shattered, too delicate to repair.

Smashed to pieces before ones' own eyes,

Damaged beyond recognition!

Crushed like a chip under a shoe,

Ground into powder and dust,

Cannot be brushed aside.

Who holds ones' hand?

Who understands grief?

Undeniable but true – blue.

The yellow is there to be seen, hidden in green.

The Sunflower shines, like a yellow gemstone,

As does a diamond buried multifaceted in rock.

B. Kay Mackle

Chances Are

The butterfly she sits and waits,

Contemplating her fate.

Why does she hesitate? Why does she wait?

She has been through many stages,

She has transformed.

She has reformed.

She has a new form,

What makes her forlorn?

She is kept in the dark,

She is kept at arms-length.

Her wings are dry,

No need for despair.

Her wings are open, not bent or broken,

Slightly damaged, in a minor way.

The tips are frayed, can't be repaired,
This is why she is so afraid to fly.
When she clears the window of her mind,
When she lets go in preparation for the new,
Transformation will take place.
Step back, pause, reflect,
Her wings will not let her down.
She will not fall to the ground.
Her legs will hold her,
Her legs will not fold.
When she is willing to let go of the past,
to embrace the future.
When she is not too weak to seek,
she must hold on to faith and be willing to take flight,
She deserves a second chance.

Angelic Ways

Praise angelic hymns, sweet humming in my listening ears,

Angels love to sing and dance it seems.

If they have the chance,

they love to spread their wings and fly at height.

You may not see their radiant crown,

Or the wheel of fire at their feet,

By chance you may hear a heartbeat,

and know it is not your own.

It could possibly be an angel close by,

Do not fear.

You may hear the door-bell softly ring,

You raise to let your visitor in,

No one seems to be there in person,

Only the wind.

A calm breeze makes you sneeze,

An angel spreading dust on your nose?

Could be I suppose.

After the rain you see a rainbow spread its shining light,

from a closed crystal pane of glass.

The angels love to swing in the early morning light,

Let them in.

You see a star blinking in the clear night sky,

It catches your eye.

The angels are saying 'Hi, Hello'

A highlight, a blessing in disguise.

By chance an angel in heaven is sent to say goodbye.

B. Kay Mackle

Elevation of Creation

Business, busyness, pride, prize;
No need for expectations.
A faze, a phrase, a craze,
a passage of doorways sends me running for protection.
Danger lurking in the darkness,
People pass me by in a dream.
Remember when past commitments and fate
bring on my heart rate?
The gate is locked, can't find the key,
Even though it has been presented to me.
Freedom out of reach,
Much more to do on this earthly plane.

Fight for justice, fight for peace, fight for love,
Find the fighting spirit.
Light prevents darkness of the soul,
Calm prevents the storm in the heart.
Strength prevents weakness in the limbs,
Find success in a variety of ways.
A time beyond is what is waiting for me,
In the stillness, the early hours, I heal, I dream,
Probable cause neglect.
What is normal? What is depth?
Swept away on the tide of time,
A new time begins on a wave of success.

Tenderness - Forgiveness
Love & Time

Preconditioned.

Time to know.

From thirst, from need, a fertile seed grows.

Digging deep to find a sweet flow of nurturing blue,

Water to cleanse and drink.

Returning to the top soil (of earth) a breakthrough of green,

Growing stronger and higher the purple tinged sky is within reach.

While searching within, love is found,

Faith has transpired.

Trust is essential,

Believe in the tiny seed that succeeds against all odds.

It grows from the tree of knowledge,

Look and see the image that it portrays,

As it continues to grow strong roots,

Accessing strength and harmony from its surrounds,

It flowers, fruits and sets seeds of new awareness.

Revealing One's Inner Child

Walking a chosen path,

Listening to a pleasing voice,

She encountered something or someone she had always missed.

Something started to stir inside her, something wonderful.

Someone she thought she had lost forever,

Someone she thought she could not connect with or hold onto.

A memory of who she once was,

A movement strong from deep inside her,

Made her look, see and feel an emotion raw and real.

A tear fell from one eye and then the other,

Tears ran down her cheeks as the connection was made.

She held out her hand,

The situation and the roll were reversed.

A soft baby's head rested on her shoulder,

The touch of a newborn delicate and fresh.

Smooth, silky hair was felt on her cheek,

The motherly love was expressed, exposed.

A connection at soul level,

She recognised her-self as a child of love, content.

Someone to hold onto forever, deep within her heart.

REVEALING SELF.

AUTHOR'S NOTE

One **soul** Journey ~ One **soul** Search ~ One **soul** Realisation

One version of truth to restore myself to being. Guided by my feelings, meditation and mantra was my way...

RA MA DA SA

SA SAY SO HUNG

I restored myself with...

OM MANI PADME HUM

I released negative karma and received enlightenment (the jewel is in the lotus). With YOGA philosophy I learned the understanding of life's purpose (truth and detachment)...

NAMASTE

With REIKI, I learned to honour all.

With the LORDS PRAYER, I gained trust and faith. I welcomed and received the wholly spirit.

I AM THAT I AM

I AM ONE SOUL

Assisting global peace...

SA TA NA MA

In life, death, infinity, rebirth.

Believe it or not, this is my way to advance my soul. To be of service. To assist the world, move towards harmony and oneness.

The written word must be heard.

As I do my best to enlighten others through my personal experiences, this book of poems is only part of my mission. My children's books send messages to you all. Not tall stories, but short stories to share, bringing light onto many of the world's issues.

AUTHOR'S TESTIMONIAL

Broken by the many storms that came her way,

She breaks, holds on by a thread of HOPE.

She was prepared and planned to mend.

Many years of dedicated effort plus tender care,

Restored her strength and FAITH,

She still grows at a steady pace.

Aware of the labour of love she endures her experiences.

She reached out her hands and heart for support.

She received a surprise gift of healing for herself.

This gift she is prepared to SHARE in KINDNESS.

The GIFT of LOVE and LIGHT

That allows comfort into the body, mind, heart, and soul of others

who are prepared to BELIEVE in TRUTH.

INTUITIVE ENERGY HEALING is now

her SERVICE to the community.

FROM THE PUBLISHER

In 'The Broken Branch Grows,' author B. Kay Mackle presents a captivating collection of poeticised writings in verse that delve into themes of love, faith, kindness, and intuitive energy healing. Drawing from her own life experiences, the author shares her spiritual gifts with you in a mesmerizing manner.

From the very first poem, you will be immersed in a world of emotion, empathy, and enlightenment. Each piece within this collection resonates with a deep sense of authenticity, inviting you to explore the intricacies of the human experience through the lens of the author's spiritual journey.

'The Broken Branch Grows,' is a must-read for anyone on a journey of self-discovery, spiritual growth, and healing. It is a book to be savoured and returned to again and again.

I wish Kay all the very best in her continued journey through authorship and congratulate her on another exceptional publication.

Crystal Leonardi
Bowerbird Publishing
www.crystalleonardi.com

www.ingramcontent.com/pod-product-compliance
Ingram Content Group Australia Pty Ltd
76 Discovery Rd, Dandenong South VIC 3175, AU
AUHW011753190325
408583AU00028B/209